NORTH AMERICAN FJ-2

PHOTO ABOVE — First XFJ-2 to fly, the third prototype, 133756. Aircraft was essentially a F-86E sans wing fence and packing four 20mm guns instead of six 50 calibre ones. Photo via Stephan Nicolav.

As noted in Naval Fighters #7, the North American FJ-1 Fury ($5.50) was the forerunner of the famous F-86 series. Although the FJ-1 proved valuable in developing jet procedures aboard carriers, its performance was inadequate when compared with the XP-86 which flew ten months after the FJ-1. Because of the successful development of the swept-wing F-86, North American initiated project NA-181 for a navalised F-86, on 30 Jan. 1951. The proposal was tendered to the Navy on 6 Feb. 1951 and accepted on 10 Feb. Contract approval came on 29 May 1951 and the mockup inspection was conducted on the 26th through the 28th of June 1951. The skipper of the FJ-1 squadron VF-51, Commander Aurand, became the project officer.

Three pre-production prototypes of the XFJ-2 were ordered by the Navy. Two aircraft (133754 and 133755) designated NA-179 were ordered on the 8th of March; the third (133756) designated NA-181 was ordered on 19 March 1951. These three aircraft were built at the Los Angeles plant, while the production aircraft were to be built at North American's Columbus factory.

XFJ-2 133754 and 133755 were essentially F-86Es that were modified for carrier operations. The modifications included a V-frame arresting hook, catapult hooks and a lengthened nose wheel. These two aircraft were also completed without armament. The modifications delayed completion of the XFJ-2's til after the first flight of the third prototype on 27 Dec. 1951. The third XFJ-2 (133756) was able to fly first because its only modification was the installation of four 20mm cannons in place of the six .50 calibre guns used on the FJ-1 and F-86. This aircraft was designated XFJ-2B. The B designation was used during this period to denote a special armament modification. The XFJ-2B was tested at Inyokern (China Lake) for armament testing.

The first XFJ-2 finally flew on 14 Feb. 1952. After initial testing, the two XFJ-2s were transferred to the Naval Air Test Center at Patuxent River, Maryland, where they underwent carrier qualification trials in Dec. 1952 aboard the USS Coral Sea.

The XFJ-2s as flown from the Coral Sea were equipped with General Electric J47-GE-13 engines. Production FJ-2s were built with GE J47-GE-2 engines of 6,000 lbs. thrust, and as such were basically equivalent to the slatted-wing F-86F. Lessons learned with the XFJ-2s were adapted to the production aircraft as well as the addition of folding wings. As a result of the armament tests conducted on the XFJ-2B, the production FJ-2s incorporated the four 20mm. guns with 600 rounds. The first control system included a AN/APG-30 radar and a Mark 16 Mod 2 gunsight.

The first production FJ-2, 131927, was accepted in Nov. 1972, but production was slow in coming as the Korean War made F-86F production at North American paramount. Only 25 FJ-2's were completed by Jan. 1954. From here production accelerated and the 200th FJ-2 was completed in Sept. 1954.

THE AIRPLANE

The JF-2 is a high-performance, single-place fighter-type airplane designed for operation from land bases or from CV-34 and CVB class carriers. It is powered by a turbo-jet engine and is characterized by swept-back wings and empennage. Noteworthy design features include combined action of elevator and stabilizer known as the controllable horizontal stabilizer, a completely irreversible hydraulic flight control system for operation of the horizontal stabilizer and ailerons, and an artificial feel system to provide stick forces simulating aerodynamic loads. In addition, the airplane has leading edge wing slats and speed brakes which are located in the right and left sides of the fuselage. Over-all dimensions of the airplane are as follows:

Wing span	37.1 feet
wings folded	22.4 feet
Length	37.6 feet
Height	13.6 feet
wings folded	15.8 feet

The airplane is armed with four Mark 12, 20mm guns which are mounted in pairs on each side of the fuselage near the air intake duct in the nose.

ENGINE

The engine is a J47-GE-2 axial-flow turbojet type with a rated sea level thrust of approximately 6000 pounds. To prevent icing, the 37 inlet guide vanes are continuously heated during engine operation. This is achieved by bleeding air from the last stage of the compressor and routing it through the vanes. Engine lubrication is provided by a recirculating, positive-displacement system that supplies lubricating oil to the various gears and engine bearings. This oil also cools the bearings and their supporting structures in the turbine frame. Scavenge pumps return the oil to the oil tank which is serviced to a level of 3.26 gallons. The ignition system utilizes a dual ignition vibrator unit which converts d-c power into high-voltage a-c power for firing the igniters in combustion chambers No. 3 and 7. This unit provides ignition voltage for both normal ground starts and emergency air starts. The combination starter-generator functions as a starter until engine speed reaches 21 to 23% rpm, after which the unit serves as a generator. The following units are driven by the engine: the utility hydraulic pump, the normal flight control hydraulic pump, the starter-generator, the tachometer generator, the engine oil pumps, a fuel pump and the governor in the fuel control regulator.

HYDRAULIC SYSTEMS

The airplane is equipped with three separate hydraulic systems: a utility hydraulic system with an emergency hydraulic system used for emergency extension of the nose gear, a flight control normal hydraulic system, and a flight control alternate hydraulic system. These systems are of the 3000 psi closed-center type. The flight control normal hdyraulic system and the flight control alternate hydraulic system supply hydraulic power for operation of the ailerons and the controllable horizontal tail. The utility hydraulic system supplies power for operation of the landing gear speed brakes, wheel brakes, wing fold, arresting hook retraction, tail bumper, nose gear catapult estension, and gun bay purge door, as well as the motor which operates the air compressor.

FLIGHT CONTROL SYSTEM

Four unique features are incorporated in the flight control system. First, the ailerons and horizontal stabilizer are completely operated by a hydraulic flight control system; movement of the control stick mechanically positions hydraulic control valves which direct pressure to the respective control surface actuating cylinders. Second, the horizontal stabilizer and the elevators are both primary control surfaces, known as the controllable horizontal stabilizer, and are jointly operated for longitudinal control through normal stick action. Third, to provide normal stick feel, an artificial feel system is built into the ailerons and horizontal stabilizer control systems. Fourth, no aileron or horizontal stabilizer trim tabs are provided; trimming is accomplished by changing the neutral position of the stick. The rudder is conventionally operated by a cable control system and has an electrically actuated trim tab.

FUEL SYSTEM

The fuel system includes five internal fuel cells and provisions for two combat-type droppable wing tanks. In addition to the normal individual filler points for each tank, a single-point refueling system is included. This system permits all internal tanks to be refueled from special ground servicing equipment through a single receptacle on the left forward side of the fuselage. A fuel level control valve, located in the forward fuselage tank, closes when the tanks are filled to capacity. This creates a back pressure within the refueling manifold, which automatically stops the incoming fuel flow at the refueling nozzle. The fuel filler access doors at the normal tank filler points cannot be closed unless the tank caps are secured in the locked position. During normal refueling operations, the forward fuselage fuel cell must be filled first to utilize full capacity of the fuel system. A fuel quantity indicating system and a fuel flowmeter are part of the fuel system. Operation of the fuel system is essentially automatic, requiring no tank selection by the pilot. When drop tanks are installed, the drop tank transfer switch should be turned to TRANSFER as soon as possible after take-off. This will assure maximum use of auxiliary fuel in the event it becomes necessary to salvo the drop tanks.

WING DROP TANKS

A 200-gallon combat-type droppable tank can be installed on each wing to increase the fuel carrying capabilities of the airplane. Fuel from these drop tanks flows into the internal fuel cells through the lines of the single-point refueling-system. The drop tank transfer switch controls the compressed air supply to the drop tanks. When the switch is in TRANSFER, fuel is forced out of the drop tanks into the internal fuel cells by air pressure from the engine compressor. Provisions are made for release of fuel from both drop tanks to permit a rapid reduction in airplane gross weight if circumstances require. This fuel jettisoning is controlled by the drop tank fuel dump switch located on the aft section of the left console.

The drop tanks themselves may be released by a button located forward of the throttle quadrant. Depressing this button releases the tanks electrically, provided the weight of the airplane is not on the gear. In the event of a malfunction in the electrical drop tank release system, both drop tanks may be jettisoned manually by pulling the drop tank emergency release handle located on the center pedestal.

WING FLAPS

Electrically controlled and operated, slotted-type wing flaps extend spanwise from the fuselage to the aileron on each wing panel. An individual electrical circuit and motor powered by the primary bus are provided to actuate each flap. The flaps are mechanically interconnected, so that if one actuating motor or electrical circuit fails, the respective flap will be actuated through mechanical linkage with the opposite flap. This mechanical interlinkage also prevents individual or uneven flap operation, and a brake coil within each actuator prevents air loads from moving the flaps.

WING SLATS

Wing slats extend from just outboard of the fuselage to the tip along the leading edge of each wing. The slats are fully automatic in operation and depending on the angle of attack move to either close, partially open, or the full open position. Upon opening, the slats move forward along a curved track to create a slot in the wing leading edge. This slot formation changes the airflow over the upper surface of the wing and increases lift, resulting in lower stalling speed. At speeds above approximately 200 knots, in unaccelerated flight, the slats remain closed to offer minimum drag for maximum flight performance.

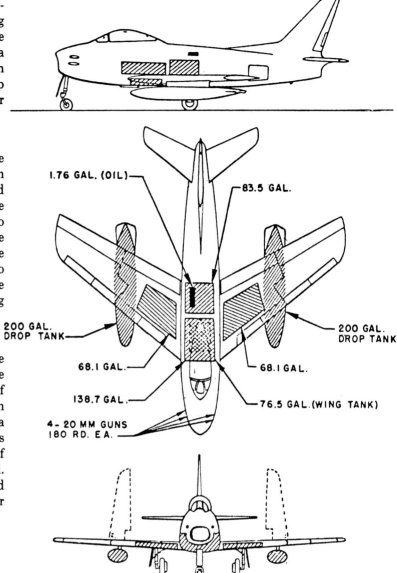

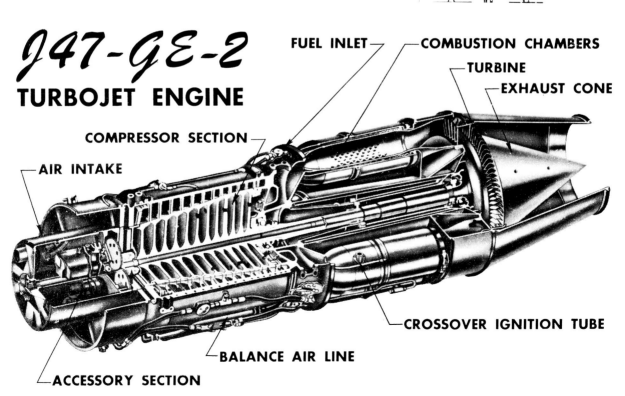

LANDING GEAR

The fully retractable tricycle landing gear and the gear and wheel fairing doors are hydraulically actuated and electrically controlled and sequenced. The main gear retracts inboard into the lower surface of the wing and the fuselage; the nose gear retracts aft into the fuselage, pivoting 90 degrees, so that the nose wheel is horizontal when retracted. After the gear is down and locked, the wheel fairing doors are retracted to the closed position to prevent mud, dirt, etc., from entering the wheel wells during ground operation. Ground safety pins are provided and should be installed when airplane is secured. A hydraulically actuated tail bumper is extended and retracted in conjunction with the landing gear and catapult holdback pendant.

WHEEL BRAKES

The wheel brakes are hydraulically operated by toe pressure on the rudder pedals. Brake pressure is supplied from the brake master cylinders, supplemented by boost power from the utility hydrualic system. If the utility hydraulic system pressure fails, the brakes will function through action of the master cylinders. There are no provisions for parking brakes.

ARRESTING GEAR

The arresting hook, located forward of the tail bumper, is extended by a combination of snubber accumulator pressure and gravity, and is retracted by utility hydraulic system pressure. When retracted, the whole arresting hook assembly, except the hook point, is completely covered by doors which fold inward when the hook is extended. No emergency provisions are included, since the hook will automatically drop if the arresting gear release cable breaks. A barrier guard and a barrier pickup are automatically released and the approach light is illuminated when the landing gear and arresting gear hook are extended and exterior light switch in ON.

BARRIER GUARD

A tubular barrier guard is located just forward of the windshield, to the right of the airplane centerline. The guard is spring-loaded to the up position and automatically extends when the arresting hook is lowered. After landing, the guard is manually returned to the retracted position, flush with the fuselage.

BARRIER PICKUP

The crash barrier pickup is in the lower surface of the fuselage, directly aft of the nose wheel well. The pickup is pivoted on the catapult hook fitting and held by a latch at the forward end. The latch is actuated, releasing the barrier pickup when the arresting gear is lowered. The barrier pickup cannot be retracted in flight. It must be retracted manually on the ground.

CATAPULT EQUIPMENT

A catapult hook and holdback fitting are provided for catapulting the airplane from a carrier deck. The fixed catapult hook is attached to the front spar of the center section; the retractable holdback fitting is located forward of the arresting gear and is covered by a fairing plate when retracterd. The holdback fitting is extended manually and is automatically retracted when the airplane is released.

WING FOLDING SYSTEM

The wing folding and spreading cycles are hydraulically operated and electrically controlled through a solenoid-operated, four-way selector valve. The control for operating the wing fold is located on the right side of the cockpit below the windshield bow. The wing fold selector value is located in the right forward fuselage and is accessible through a door marked "HYDRAULIC EQUIPMENT." A button on the lock and dump valve can be depressed to allow the ground crew to spread the wings manually.

SPEED BRAKES

Hydraulically operated speed brakes are located on each side of the fuselage below the dorsal fin. Each speed brake consists of a panel hinged at the forward edge which, when open, extends into the air stream. Pressure for normal operation of the speed brakes is supplied by the utility hydraulic system. An emergency control is provided to close the speed brakes. With high speed or dive conditions, the opening time is approximately 4 seconds. A barber-pole-type position indicator on the left console forward of the quadrant will show OUT for full open position, a barber pole for intermediate position, and IN for closed position.

PHOTO ABOVE — Speed brake detail. Interior was originally red, but later became zinc chromate with silver tubing and cylinders and black rubber hoses.

MAJOR FJ-1 SOURCE MATERIAL

1. Air Classics. August 1974, "Fury At Sea", Robert Trimble.
2. Profile Publications Number 42, The North American FJ Fury. 1965, Francis K. Mason.
3. The North American Sabre. 1963, MacDonald & Co., Ray Wagner.

CONTRIBUTORS

ROGER BESECKER, JIM BURRIDGE, HONDO FRAIN, DUDLEY GILLASPY, CLAY JANSSON, "MULE" HOLMBERG, RICK KOEHNEN, LEO KOHN, BOB KOWALSKI, WILLIAM LARKINS, ROBERT LAWSON, DAVE MENARD, STEPHANE NICOLAOU, RON PICCIANI, WILLIAM SWISHER AND NICK WILLIAMS.

PHOTOS: TOP AND BOTTOM — Two routine ground views of XFJ-2B (133756) at NAS Patuxent River, Maryland, on 18 Aug. 1953. Plane was attached to the Armament Test Division of NATC at the time. Note F-86 drop-tanks, landing gear and canopy. Note location and size of ammunition doors and gun ports and how they differ from the F-86. National Archives photos.

MIDDLE PHOTO — North American engineering test pilot Robert Hoover points to a belt of 20 mm ammunition being shown him by Armorer Donald Beuter. Ammunition on Beuter's left shoulder is 50 calibre. Note white stenciling on the blue paint and the step location. NASM photo. Also note in these three photos the F-86 style dyhedral which only appeared on the XFJ-2s and not on the production FJ-2s.

ARMAMENT EQUIPMENT

The armament equipment consists of four Mark 12, 20mm guns and an Aero 10B, 10F or 10F-1 armament control system.

GUNNERY EQUIPMENT

The Mark 12, 20mm guns are mounted in pairs; one pair is located in the left gun bay, the other pair in the right gun bay. A pneumatic system provides air pressure for gun charging and pressure for the pneumatic feeder. The ammunition boost system is electrically operated. A gun bay purging system is provided to clear the gun bays of smoke and explosive gases that may accumulate.

ARMAMENT CONTROL SYSTEM (AERO 01B, 10F or 10F-1)

The armament control system is an automatic lead-computing, pilot-operated system for aiming the fixed guns. The system eliminates guess work in determining velocity, range, and other variables encountered in tracking a target.

RADAR EQUIPMENT (AN/APG-30 OR AN/ APG-30A)

The AN/APG-30 radar equipment is an automatic range measuring device. The equipment consists of a microwave transmitter, an antenna, a receiver, and a range measuring circuit. The transmitter generates a search impulse which is radiated from the antenna. The receiver detects and amplifies refleted impulses which are picked up by the antenna. In the absence of a target, the radar will search in the range selected by the control marked "MAX RANGE" on the control panel. When a target is detected, the tracking gate "locks on" and stays "locked on" the target as long as the target moves within detection range of the search cone. The operating range of the radar is 225 to 3000 yards.

PHOTO BELOW — Gun camera modification of FJ-2 cockpit, 131975, at MCAS El Toro, Calif., 18 March 1954.

armament controls and indicators

RANGE METER

MARK 11 MOD 1 SIGHT UNIT

ON-TARGET INDICATOR LIGHT

RANGE SWITCH

AIRPLANES 131930 THROUGH 132226

AIRPLANES 131927 THROUGH 131929

UNCAGE GYRO

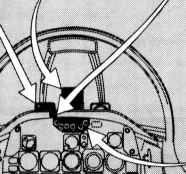
AIRPLANES 131927 THROUGH 131938

AIRPLANES 131939 THROUGH 132226

GUN CONTROL PANEL

CIRCUIT-BREAKERS

TRIGGER SWITCH
SIGHT UNIT ADJUSTMENTS
FIXED RETICLE MASKING KNOB
CRYSTAL CURRENT METER

RADAR CONTROL PANEL

FIRE CONTROL PANEL

AIRPLANES HAVING SERVICE CHANGE NO. 85 COMPLIED WITH

H-181-61-42A

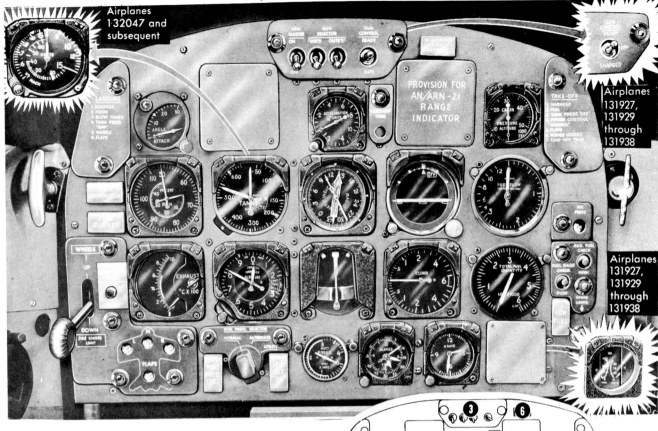

1. Landing Check List
2. Angle-of-attack Indicator
3. Gun Control Panel
4. Accelerometer
5. Take-off Trim Indicator
6. Windshield Overheat Warning Light
7. Cabin Pressure Altitude Indicator
8. Take-off Check List
9. Fire Detection Lights
10. Tachometer
11. Airspeed Indicator
12. Radio Magnetic Course Indicator
13. Attitude Horizon Indicator
14. Fuel Flowmeter
15. Oil Pressure Indicator
16. Landing Gear Control
17. Fire Detector Test Switch
18. Tail-pipe Temperature Indicator
19. Altimeter
20. Turn-and-bank Indicator
21. Rate-of-climb Indicator
22. Fuel Quantity Indicator
23. Fuel Gage Check Switch
24. Auxiliary Fuel Check Switch
25. Landing Gear and Flap Position Indicator
26. Nose Gear Stiff Indicator Light
27. Hydraulic Pressure Selector
28. Hydraulic Alternate System "ON" Light
29. Hydraulic Pressure Indicator
30. Elapsed-time Clock
31. Clock
32. Voltammeter
33. Low Fuel Level Warning Light
34. Canopy Emergency Release Handle
35. Landing Gear Emergency Release Handle

instrument panel

cockpit right side

1. Utility receptacle
2. Wing fold control
3. Cockpit light
4. Battery and generator switch
5. Generator warning light
6. Arresting hook control
7. Exterior lighting control panel
8. Instrument power switch
9. Inverter warning light
10. UHF control panel
11. Circuit-breaker panel
12. Interior light rheostat
13. Radio compass control panel
14. Interior light control panel
15. Warning light test switch
16. IFF control panel
17. Anti-ice and defrost panel
18. Gyrosyn compass control panel

cockpit-left side

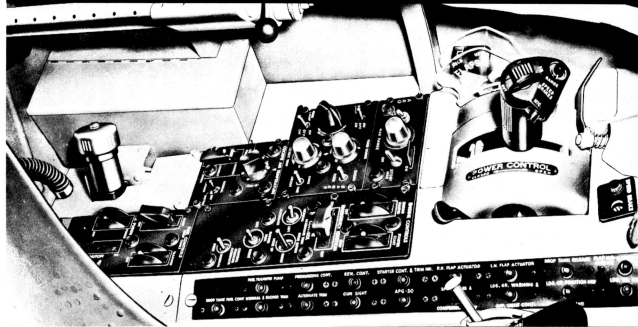

1. Map case
2. Cabin air deflector control
3. Wing flap control
4. Anti-G suit regulator valve
5. Cockpit air temperature control panel
6. Fire control panel
7. Radar control panel
8. Throttle
9. Throttle catapult handle
10. Fuel shutoff control
11. Fuel purge switch
12. Drop tank transfer switch
13. Drop tank fuel dump switch
14. Flight control system selector switch
15. Rudder trim switch
16. Stabilizer-aileron alternate trim switch
17. Trim control selector switch
18. Emergency ignition switch
19. Engine master switch
20. Starter start-stop switch
21. Throttle friction lock
22. Speed brake position indicator
23. Circuit-breaker panel
24. Shoulder-harness release lever

LANDING
1. FUEL TRANSFER
2. BLOW TANKS
3. HARNESS
4. HOOK PRESS OFF
5. WHEELS -205Kn
6. FLAPS -205Kn

CHECK LISTS

TAKE-OFF
1. FUEL
2. FUEL TRANSFER
3. WINGS
4. POWER CONTROL
5. TRIM
6. FLAPS
7. HARNESS
8. OXYGEN

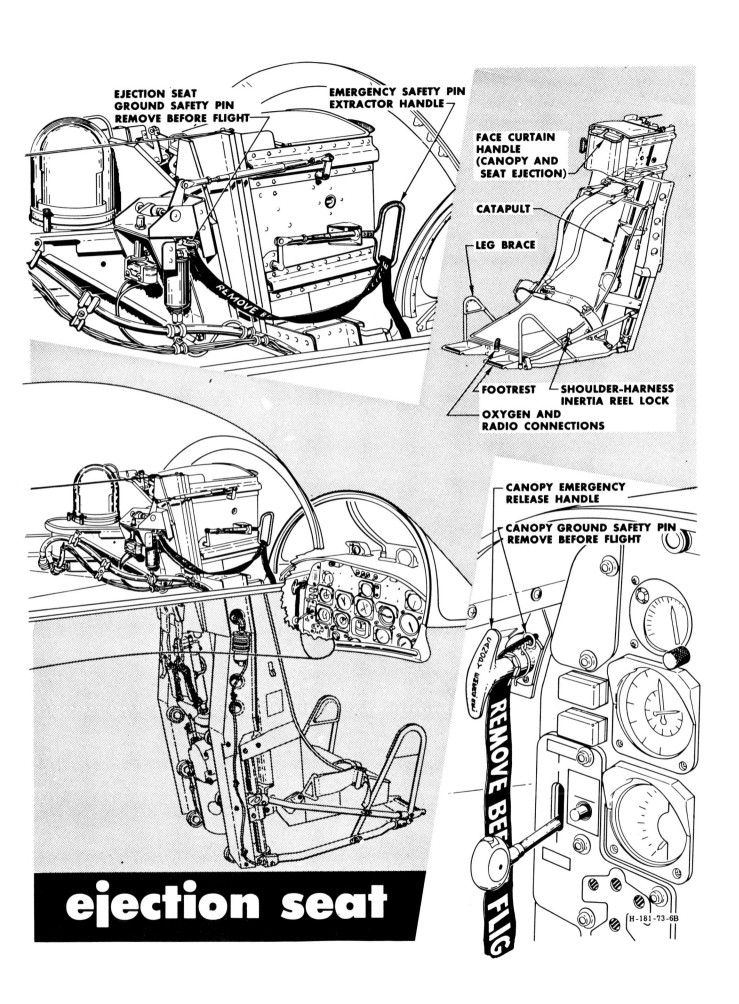

TABLE OF COMMUNICATION AND ASSOCIATED ELECTRONIC EQUIPMENT

TYPE	DESIGNATION	FUNCTION	RANGE	LOCATION OF CONTROLS
UHF TRANSCEIVER	AN/ARC-27A	Ultra-high frequency two-way voice communication between airplanes or between airplanes and ground stations	Line of sight	Right console
UHF DIRECTION FINDING EQUIPMENT	AN/ARA-25	Ultra-high frequency air-to-air or air-to-ground direction finding	Line of sight	Right console
RADIO COMPASS	AN/ARN-6	Low frequency and medium frequency receiving and direction finding	Dependent on atmospheric conditions	Right console
RADIO NAVIGATION RECEIVER	AN/ARN-21	Reception of ultra-high frequency omni-range and voice facilities*	Line of sight	Right console
IFF EQUIPMENT	AN/APX-6 AND AN/APA-89	Automatic identification	Line of sight	Right console
RADAR EQUIPMENT	AN/APG-30 (or AN/APG-30A)	Furnishes range information to the aircraft fire control system	225 to 3000 yards	Left console

ENTERING THE COCKPIT

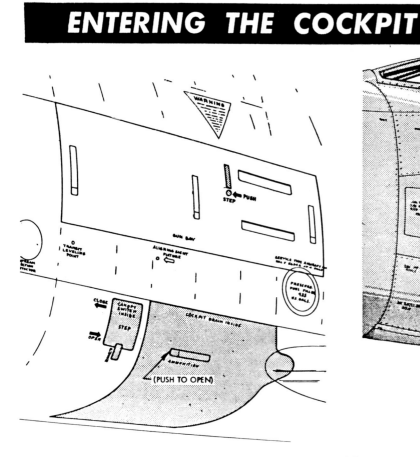

FJ-2-1-00-3A

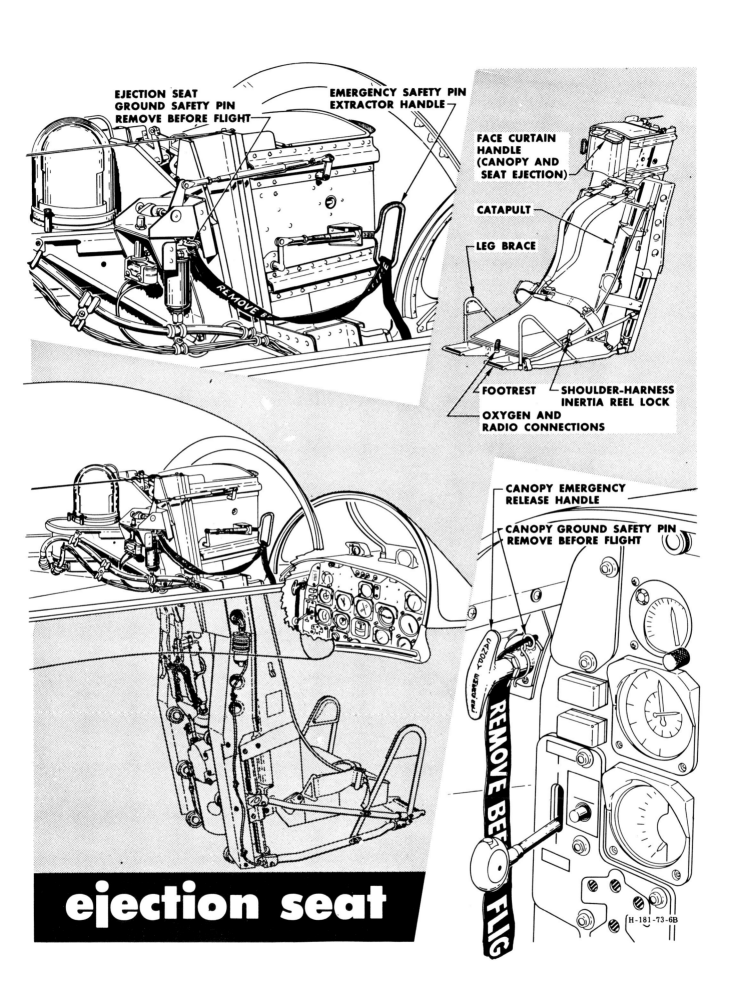

TABLE OF COMMUNICATION AND ASSOCIATED ELECTRONIC EQUIPMENT

TYPE	DESIGNATION	FUNCTION	RANGE	LOCATION OF CONTROLS
UHF TRANSCEIVER	AN/ARC-27A	Ultra-high frequency two-way voice communication between airplanes or between airplanes and ground stations	Line of sight	Right console
UHF DIRECTION FINDING EQUIPMENT	AN/ARA-25	Ultra-high frequency air-to-air or air-to-ground direction finding	Line of sight	Right console
RADIO COMPASS	AN/ARN-6	Low frequency and medium frequency receiving and direction finding	Dependent on atmospheric conditions	Right console
RADIO NAVIGATION RECEIVER	AN/ARN-21	Reception of ultra-high frequency omni-range and voice facilities*	Line of sight	Right console
IFF EQUIPMENT	AN/APX-6 AND AN/APA-89	Automatic identification	Line of sight	Right console
RADAR EQUIPMENT	AN/APG-30 (or AN/APG-30A)	Furnishes range information to the aircraft fire control system	225 to 3000 yards	Left console

ENTERING THE COCKPIT

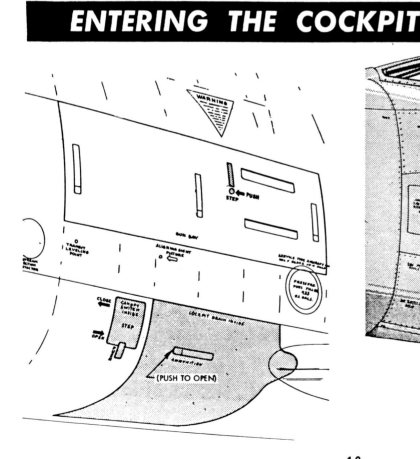

exterior inspection

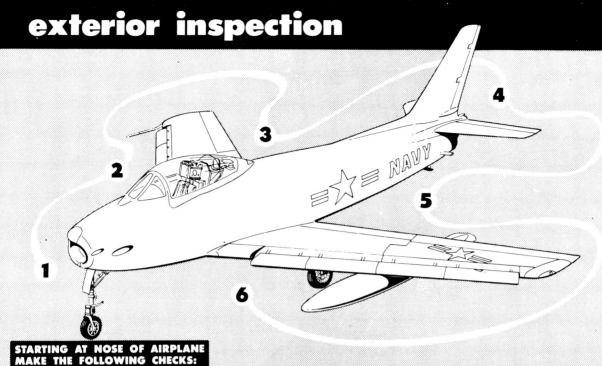

STARTING AT NOSE OF AIRPLANE MAKE THE FOLLOWING CHECKS:

① nose
- Nose gear ground safety lock removed.
- Nose gear oleo strut extension, tire for slippage and proper inflation, main wheels chocked, hydraulic leaks.
- Intake duct clear, approach light.
- Access doors secure.

② forward fuselage and right wing leading edge
- Gun camera.
- Slats free.
- Fuel cap secure (wing).
- Drop tank secure and undamaged, fuel caps secure.
- Fuel cell leaks.
- Pitot tube uncovered, position light.
- Access doors secure.

③ right wing trailing edge and aft fuselage
- Aileron and flap secure.
- Landing gear ground safety pin removed.
- Security of landing gear doors, strut extension, hydraulic leaks, tires for slippage and proper inflation.
- Fuel cap secure (fuselage).
- Arresting gear retracted and secure.
- Aileron lock removed.
- Access doors secure.

④ empennage
- Rudder trim tab secure.
- Position light.
- Tail-pipe plug removed, tail pipe for cracks or excessive distortion.

⑤ left wing trailing edge and aft fuselage
- Landing gear ground safety pin removed.
- Security of landing gear doors, strut extension, hydraulic leaks, tires for slippage and proper inflation.
- Aileron and flap secure.
- Access doors secure.
- Aileron lock removed.

⑥ left wing leading edge and forward fuselage
- Position light.
- Drop tank secure and undamaged, fuel caps secure.
- Fuel caps secure (wing and fuselage).
- Fuel cell leaks.
- Slats free.
- Access doors secure.
- Airstream detector cover removed.

H-181-00-29B

FLIGHT TESTING THE FJ-2
Captain Robert F. Dreesen, USN, ret., as told to Jim Burridge

Captain Dreesen flew many of the Navy's second generation of jet fighters while assigned to NAS Patuxent River in the early 1950's. (See Naval Fighters Number Six for his account of test flying the Cutlass.)

Dreesen was introduced to the FJ-2 rather late in its test program, while he was assigned to the Armament Test Directorate, and he logged about 30 flights in the aircraft. There were two problems with the Fury's gun armament system with which he had to deal. One was solved easily, but the second was never resolved and greatly limited the FJ-2's air-to-air combat capability.

The FJ-2 was the first Navy fighter to use electric-primed ammunition guns. The spent cartridges were ejected from slots behind the guns, near the leading edges of the wings. Under a significant number of flight conditions, the spent cartridges were picked up by the airflow and would strike the rear fuselage area and elevators — sometimes even impacting on the tops of the elevators. The problem had been discovered long before Dreesen encountered the Fury, and his task was to check North American's solution. The company had carved out a storage area for the shells below and behind the guns. Testing had to be done to make sure that there was no explosive accumulation of gun gas in the storage area. The second task was to ensure that the storage area didn't fill up so rapidly that the guns jammed.

The spent cartridge problem was thus resolved, but the second problem was to prove more intractable. For all preceding prop fighters and the first generation of Navy jet fighters, the gun line was zero — that is, right down the roll axis of the aircraft. When pulling G's and trying to put lead on a target — say, 50 to 100 mils on the gunsight — the aiming point would be below the roll axis. But the pilot learns where his roll axis is and learns to compensate for it while maneuvering and tracking a target.

But somebody — presumably the Navy project officer in the Bureau of Aeronautics — thought he had a better idea. This individual thought that it would be neat if the gun axis corresponded to the actual aiming point for a certian set of "average" air combat flight conditions. In other words, under this set of conditions — say, a three G turn at 35,000 feet at 500 knots with a medium fuel load — the zero lead aiming point would correspond with the roll axis. In order to achieve this correspondence under this predetermined set of flight condicondence, the gun line was angled down. The hitch was that for all *other* conditions of airspeed, altitude, G force, and weight, the aiming point was way below the roll axis. All the aiming points formed a sort of pendulum below the roll axis. If you were tracking a turning aircraft with the gun sight on him, the gun sight line would rotate around a different axis from the aiming point — hence the pendulem effect. A normal rolling maneuver in other aircraft would allow the pilot to keep the aiming point on target, but in the FJ-2 you had to constantly raise or lower the nose while rolling because you were trying to position the end of a swinging pendulum on the target.

Dreesen and his section chief in Armament Test, Commander (now Rear Admiral, retired) Paul Pugh, worked up a series of canned tracking exercises to establish to the Bureau of Aeronautics that this innovation was not only not an advantage, but a serious problem. In the drills, experienced and new jet pilots maneuvered the Fury and several other Navy jets against target aircraft. The exercises consisted basically of turns, pullups, and rolls in the one to three G range. Each pilot flew all the different tracking aircraft to determine the degree of difficulty for each in keeping the guns on a maneuvering target. According to Dreeson, "the FJ-2 was a disaster in comparison to other fighters of significantly lower performance."

By the time the report was finished and submitted, it was even too late to correct the problem for the production FJ-3, much less for the FJ-2. So the FJ-2 went to the fleet — to the Marines, basically — with this serious problem unresolved.

Dreesen also noted that the FJ-2 was rather late in reaching operational status. The Air Force had taken delivery of the first F-86A's in May 1948, only seven months after the initial delivery of the straight-wing FJ-1 to the Navy. But the initial deliveries of the FJ-2 didn't take place until October 1952. The difference was that while the Air Force developed and deployed the swept-wing F-86 more or less simultaneously with its first-generation straight-wing (F-80 and F-84) fighters, the Navy built an entire generation of straight-wing jets first — the FH-1 Phantom, the FJ-1 Fury, the Banshee, and the Panther. The FJ-2, Dreesen laments, "should have been contemporary with the F-86."

PHOTO ABOVE — 11th production FJ-2 dubbed YFJ-2 belonging to System Test Division at NATC. Photo by R.F. Besecker.

PHOTO ABOVE — 5th production FJ-2, 131931, which became the FJ-3 prototype when it was fitted with a Wright J-65 engine. The nose intake of FJ-3 would be enlarged over the FJ-2 one shown here.

CARRIER SUITABILITY

PHOTO ABOVE — Flight test FJ-2 on 26 July 1954, conducting carrier suitability test aboard the USS HANCOCK (CVA-19). Pilot LCDR.C.M. Cruse had just launched from the starboard catapult. Aircraft is blue with natural metal leading edges and white markings. USN/Tailhook photo

Although the FJ-2 was the hottest aircraft entering the fleet at the time, it entered service with the Marines and not the Navy because it was deemed unsuitable for carrier operations. The initial tests with the XFJ-2s were proved less than satisfying. Since the Navy had hopes of fielding the FJ-2 in Korea, the decision was made to equip the Marines first and then solve the carrier problems.

Before the first FJ-2 was even delivered to the Navy, North American signed a contract to produce a better Fury, the FJ-3, on 18 April 1952. This contract cut the procurement of FJ-2s from 300 to 200 and insured that the Marines would be its only users.

Even though the Marines were to be the sole users of the dash two, they had to solve its sea-going discrepencies so that the FJ-3 fury could become a viable force with the fleet. The fourth FJ-2, 131930, was detailed to this task. This aircraft was beefed up based on the results of the earlier XFJ-2 tests and then tested. The tests were not satisfactory because of the inability of the arresting hook bumper support structure to withstand loads imposed in low sink, nose high, free flight arrested landings. The arresting hook bumper support structure was subsequently modified and new tests were conducted aboard the USS Hancock (CVA-19) in July 1954. Not only was 131930 modified, but four operational FJ-2s from VMF-235 were also modified. These were 131979, 131996, 131998 and 132003. The tests were conducted off San Diego with many other fleet aircraft which included: F3D-2Ms of VX-4, F7U-3s of VF-124, and F9F-6s of VF-24. The results again showed the FJ-2 unsuitable for carrier operations until adequate strength be provided in the arresting hook bumper support structure and the nose gear. This conclusion was the result of the dash two's experiencing five arresting hook bumper failures and two nose gear fork failures. Three bumper failures ocurred in 132003, one in 131998 and one in 131996. The nose gear forks failed once in 131930 and once in 131979.

AMERICAN AVIATION HISTORICAL SOCIETY
P. O. BOX 99,
GARDEN GROVE,
CA 92642

PHOTOS on these two pages show the two XFJ-2 aircraft 133754 and 133755 which were essentially navalized F-86Es. **AT LEFT** — 133754, note tail skid extended and flotation bag fixed to lower wing-tip. **BELOW MIDDLE** — 754 again, testing catapult holdback gear, note white X has been added to fuselage. **BOTTOM** - 744 and 755 being readied for take-off on the flight deck of the USS Midway (CVB-41), on 19 Sept. 1952. Note large numbers on nose gear doors. **AT RIGHT TOP** — 744 and 755 on the flight deck of the USS Coral Sea (CVA-43), in Nov. 1952. **AT RIGHT BOTTOM** — Deck handlers readying 755 for launch from the Coral Sea. Note stenciling locations, pilot in full up position and silver nose gear.

18

CARRIER LANDING PATTERN — GROSS WEIGHT—15,000 POUNDS

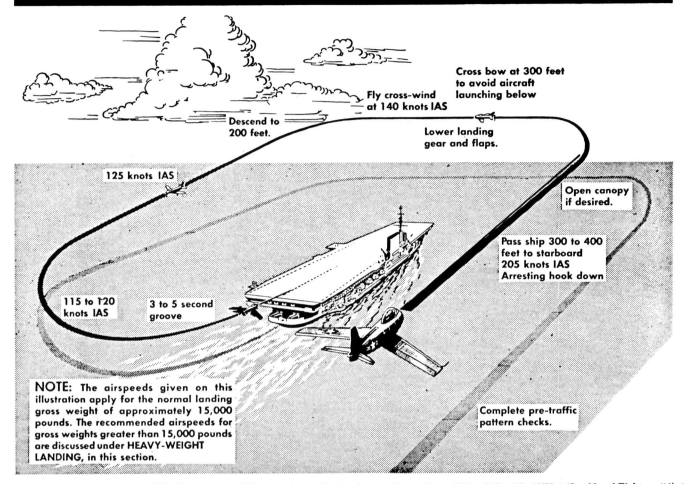

PHOTO BELOW — Deck of the USS Hancock on 15 July 1954 during Project Steam Flight. Note all blue F3D-2M of VX-4 (See Naval Fighters #4), two F7U-3 Cutlasses from VF-124 (see Naval Fighters #6), NATC FJ-2 131930, and two VMF-235 FJ-2s (#22 is 131979). National Archives photo.

19

PERFORMANCE SUMMARY		
TAKE-OFF LOADING CONDITION		(1) FIGHTER 2 - 200 Gal. Tanks External
TAKE-OFF WEIGHT	lb.	18,882
Fuel (Fixed/Drop)	lb.	2,610/2,400
Payload (Ammunition)	lb.	405
Wing loading	lb./sq.ft.	65.5
Stall speed - power-off	kn.	112.5
Take-off run at S.L. - calm	ft.	2,800
Take-off run at S.L. 25 kn. wind	ft.	1,850
Take-off to clear 50 ft. - calm		—
Max. speed/altitude (1)	kn./ft.	530/S.L.
Rate of climb at S.L. (1)	fpm	4,700
Time: S.L. to 20,000 ft. (1)	min.	6.1
Time: S.L. to 30,000 ft. (1)	min.	12.7
Service ceiling (100 fpm) (1)	ft.	37,000
Combat range	n.mi.	1,040
Average cruising speed	kn.	460
Cruising altitude(s)	ft.	37,300/45,400
Combat radius	n.mi.	395
Average cruising speed	kn.	452
COMBAT LOADING CONDITION		(2) CLEAN
COMBAT WEIGHT	lb.	16,122
Engine power		Military
Fuel	lb.	2,610
Combat speed/combat altitude	kn./ft.	521/35,000
Rate of climb/combat altitude	fpm/ft.	1,800/35,000
Combat ceiling (500 fpm)	ft.	43,000
Rate of climb at S.L.	fpm	8,050
Max. speed at S.L.	kn.	596
Max. speed/altitude	kn./ft.	596/S.L.
LANDING WEIGHT	lb.	14,013
Fuel	lb.	501
Stall speed - power-off	kn.	96.8
Stall speed - with approach power	kn.	91.2

Performance calculations are based on the following average J47-GE-27 engine ratings:

NOTES
(1) Normal Power

	Lbs.	@ Rpm	@ Alt.
T.O.	6,090	7,950	S.S.L.
MIL.	6,090	7,950	S.S.L.
NORMAL	5,590	7,630	S.S.L.

POWER PLANT
NO. & MODEL......(1) J47-GE-2
MFR......General Electric
TYPE......Axial Flow
ENG. LENGTH......144"
ENG. DIAMETER......40"

RATINGS
	Lbs.	@ Rpm	@ Alt.
T.O.	6,000	7,950	S.S.L.
MIL.	6,000	7,950	S.S.L.
NORMAL	5,270	7,630	S.S.L.

DIMENSIONS
WING AREA......288 sq. ft.
SPAN......37' - 1"
LENGTH......37' - 7"
HEIGHT......13' - 7"
TREAD......9' - 0"
M.A.C.......8' - 1"

WEIGHTS
Loadings	Lbs.	L.F.
EMPTY	12,275	
BASIC	12,800	
DESIGN	16,482	6.5
COMBAT	16,122	6.5
MAX.T.O. (Field)	18,882*	5.2
MAX.LAND.(Field)	18,882	

All weights are estimated.
*Maximum anticipated loading.

FUEL AND OIL
Gal.	No. Tanks	Location
213	3	Wing
222	2	Fuselage
400	2	Wing, Drop

FUEL GRADE......100/130
FUEL SPEC...MIL-F-5572

OIL
CAPACITY (Gals.)......3.2
GRADE......1010
SPEC......MIL-O-6081

ELECTRONICS
UHF TRANSMTR-REC...AN/ARC-27A
UHF ADF......AN/ARA-25
ADF......AN/ARN-6
RADIO ALTIMETER......AN/APN-1
 or AN/APN-22
IFF TRANSPONDOR......AN/APX-6
RADAR......AN/APG-30
ADF......AN/ARN-21
(Replacement for AN/ARN-6)

ORDNANCE
GUNS
No.	Size	Location	Rds.
4	20 mm	Fuse. Fwd.	720

FIRE CONTROL
A.F.C.S......Mk. 16 Mod. 0
Radar Ranging Equipment
......AN/APG-30

PHOTOS ABOVE: Factory fresh Marine FJ-2s. **TOP** — 131942, seen at a open house. Note one wing-tank is blue. **MIDDLE** — Note wings folded position and the black area above the intake which covers the APG-30. **BOTTOM** — 132087, note upper portion of vertical fin is painted light grey. Photos via Leo Kohn.

Tailhook Association
Box 40
Bonita, CA 92002

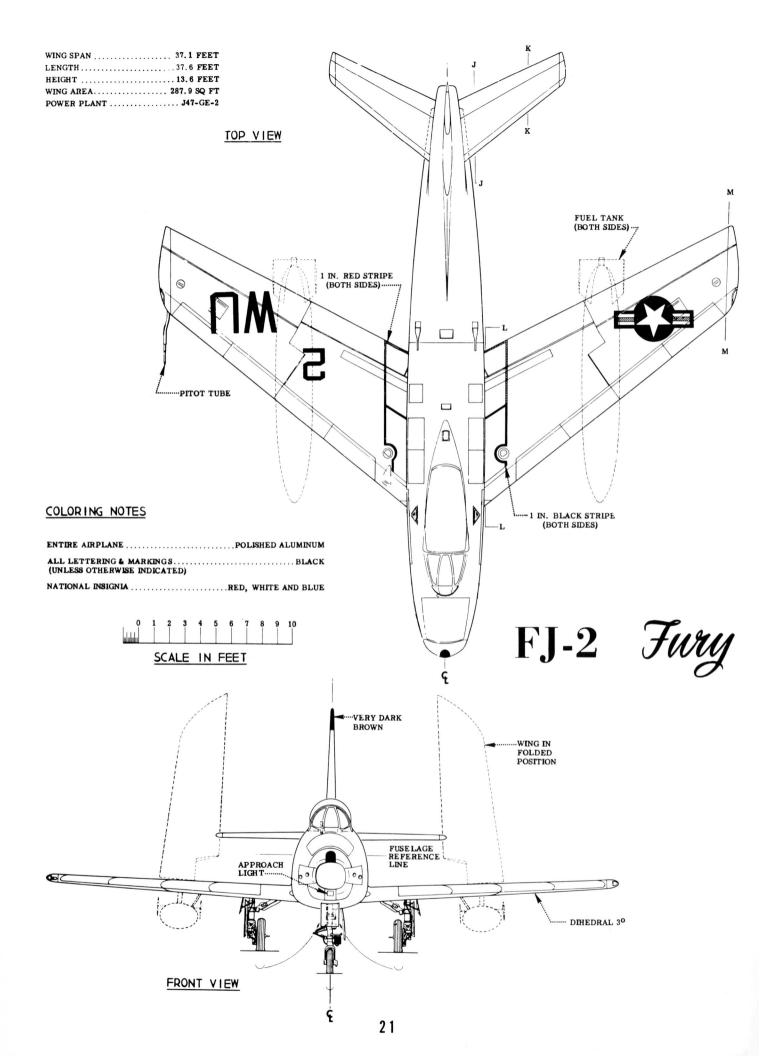

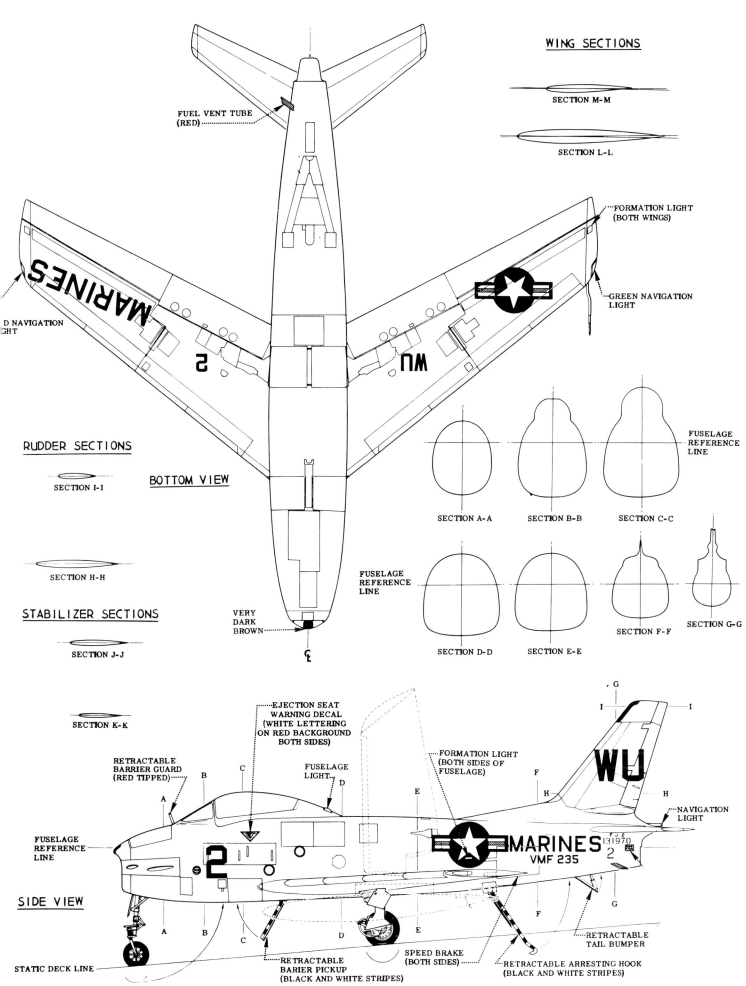

PHOTOS ABOVE AND AT LEFT —FJ-2, 131941, in flight sans squadron markings. Note on photo at left the partially opened speed brakes and the location of MARINES under the wing. USMC PHOTOS. **BELOW** — An unmarked Marine FJ-2 is catapulted into an overcast sky. Note catapult bridle is held in place by a bungee cord, so that the Fury can go back around and land and use it again. AHS photo.

Operationally the FJ-2 would be operated by six Marine squadrons; VMF-122, VMF-232, VMF-235, VMF-312, VMF-334, and VMF-451.

VMF-122

VMF-122 was the first fleet squadron to deploy the FJ-2 Fury. The Fury replaced the squadrons F9F-5 Panthers in Jan. 1954. Maj. Johnny Vance was CO of VMF-122 when the FJ-2 arrived.

Maj. Vance and his executive officer Maj. Tom Billings, had spent hours planning a schedule which called for 1,000 hours of flight time a month. Two watches, each with two sections, were organized to keep one-fourth of the squadron aloft as long as weather permitted. In this way each pilot usually got at least one flight per day.

From their home base at MCAS Cherry Point, the Candystripers, as the squadron was called, deployed aboard the USS Coral Sea (CV-43) as part of CVG-17 from March to Sept. 1955. Upon their return from the Mediterranean the squadron upgraded to the FJ-3 Fury.

VMF-122 was commissioned on 1 March 1942 and flew the F4F Wildcat. The squadron would go on to fly the F4U-1, FG-1D, and the F4U-4 Corsairs as well as the FH-1 Phantom, F2H Banshee, F6F-5 Hellcat, F9F-4 and F9F-5 Panthers and the FJ-2 and FJ-3 Furys. In Jan. 1958 the squadron changed its name to the Crusaders when it was equipped with the F8U-1 (F8A) and later the F-8E. On 1 July 1965 VMF-122 became VMFA-122 with the change to the F-4B Phantom. The squadron was to re-equip with the new F-14A in 1974 but received F-4Js in 1975 instead.

FJ-2s assigned to VMF-122: 131939, 131940, 131942, 131944, 131946, 131947, 131949, 131951-131957, 131959-131961, 131963, 131967-131969, 131984, 131985, 132049, 132060, 132062, 132067, 132076, 132073, 132077, 132080, 132081, 132090 and 132125.

ABOVE — Squadron patch 1954-1957, stripes around border were red and gold, just like on the aircraft. **PHOTO AT LEFT** — Engine check on the J-47 being conducted by Pfc. Lark, TSgt. Langdon and SSgt. Clark of VMF-122. Photo via Hondo Frain. **PHOTO BELOW** — VMF-122, FJ-2, 131951, in flight over Cherry Point. USMC photo.

PHOTOS: TOP AND AT LEFT — Two USMC photos of FJ-2, 131961 (1/LC), and 131947 (2/LC). Aircraft are natural metal with gold and red stripes and a red nose. Note windshield wipers and location of upper-wing code in the photo at left. **BELOW** — VMF-122 FJ-2 being directed forward by arresting gear chief after just landing aboard the USS Coral Sea (CVA-43) on 20 April 1955. National Archives photo.

PHOTOS: TOP — VMF-122 FJ-2, with wings folded on the squadron's line. **BOTTOM** — VMF-122 prepares to launch a flight of FJ-2s from CVA-43 in 1955. Note the two different styles of upper-wing codes used as well as the extended leading edge slats.

VMF-232

The original Red Devil squadron was activated on 1 Sept. 1925 as Division 1, Fighting Plane Squadron 3M (VF-3M) at NAS San Diego, Calif.

The units designation went through many changes before becoming VMF-232. These designations were; VF-3M, VF-10M, VF-6M, VF-10M, VB-4M, VMB-2, VMSB-232, VMTB-232, and then VMF-232 on 3 June 1948. VMF-232 would change to VMF(AW)-232 and finally VMFA-232.

The squadrons first aircraft was the Vought VE-7SF. The unit would go on to fly Boeing FB-1s, FB-5s F4B-4s, Curtiss F6C-4s, Great Lake BG-1s, Douglas SBDs, Grumman TBF-1s, F6Fs, Chance Vought F4Us, Grumman F9Fs, North American FJ-2s, FJ-4s, Chance Vought F-8s, and McDonnell F-4s.

VMF-232 flew the FJ-2 Fury from MCAS Kaneohe Bay, Hawaii, from 1955 through 1956. The dash 2 was replaced by the FJ-4 Fury in early 1957.

FJ-2s assigned to VMF-232: 131966, 131970, 131999, 132017, 132020- 132025, 132087, 132098, 132099, 132028-132032, 132035, 132039-132041, 132101, 132103, 132112, 132115, 132121, 132123 132124.

PHOTO BELOW — Four VMF-232 FJ-2s in flight. Note aircraft do not have their red stripes in this photo. AHS photo.

PHOTOS: ABOVE — VMF-232 FJ-2s in full markings off the coast of Hawaii. Note lower two, 20 and 17, are in natural metal finish with red stripes and red nose. The upper two are in grey and white scheme, #1 has a blue drop-tank and #8 has buro #'s on the tail (31999). Also note location of upper wing-codes. NASM photo. **BELOW** — VMF-232 FJ-2, 132832, taxiing at its home base MCAS Kaneohe Bay, Hawaii. Note brand new appearance of the metal and the shape of the nose flash, which is red. Photo via W.T. Larkins.

PHOTOS: ABOVE — VMF-232 FJ-2 in storage in June of 1957. Note wing brace and powder stains around gun ports. W.T. Larkins photo. **AT LEFT** — VMF-232 FJ-2, returning to dust. Note access panel locations. Leo Kohn photo. **BOTTOM** — another FJ-2 returning to dust, and with flames no less. W.T. Larkins photo.

VMF-235

During the more than 25 years of her existence, the men of Marine All Weather Fighter Attack Squadron 235, have earned the nickname of "The Death Angels." In hot and cold wars, they have lived up to their grim motto, "Ride Nunch" or "Laugh Now", and in Vietnam they made their insignia, a death angel with blood dripping sword, a symbol of death to the Viet Cong.

Commissioned on 1 January 1943, the squadron served four tours in the Pacific during World War II, participating primarily in bombing and scouting missions over Guadalcanal, Rabaul, and New Britain. Flying the Douglas SBD dive bomber, the Death Angels were commended twice for outstanding performance under enemy fire.

From the end of World War II until the outbreak of the Korean Conflict, the squadron was relegated to the Marine Air Reserve Training Command. When fighting broke out in Korea, the squadron was recalled to active duty, equipped with F4U-4 Corsairs, and sent to Marine Corps Air Station, El Toro, California. The Death Angels, while equipped with the F9F Panther Jet, from 1952 through 1954 alternated between El Toro and Kaneohe Bay, Hawaii. In 1954 the squadron received the FJ-2 Fury and was deployed to NAS, Atsugi, Japan until 1957.

When the FJ-2 arrived at MCAS El Toro, Calif., the squadron was ready for them. Colonel Sapp, World War II double ace and Navy Cross winner, had carefully organized a program which gave each pilot in his outfit six familiarization flights the first month the Furys were on his flight line. The high experience level of the maintenance crews and pilots made the transition easy. In addition to Navy Cross winners Col. Sapp, Maj. Bob Klingman, Maj. Frank (Red) Thomas, Capt. Robert (Ding) Wade, and Maj. Glenn (Dad) Riley, most of the pilots of VMF-235 had more than 2,000 hours flight time.

Marine Corps Air Station, Beaufort, South Carolina, became home to the Death Angels during the years 1957 to 1962 where they flew the Chance Vought F8 Crusader. 1963 to 1970 would see 235 flying their F-8s in Vietnam. After returning to MCAS Kaneohe Bay, they transitioned to the F-4J Phantom.

PHOTO BELOW — Early photo of VMF-235 FJ-2s prior to the adding of their colorful markings. Photo via Clay Jannson.

PHOTOS: ABOVE — The busy busy VMF-235 flightline. 24 FJ-2s in Oct. 1954. Aircraft now have their distinctive red bands with white stars. Photo by Nemile via Clay Jannson. **BELOW** — "Man your aircraft." FJ-2 131980 (10/WU) at MCAS El Toro, Calif. in Oct. 1954. NAA Tailhook VF-02940 photo.

FJ-2s assigned to VMF-235: 131958, 131965, 131970-131972, 131975-131977, 131979-131981, 131986-131992, 131996-131998, 132000, 132002, 132003, 132015, 132027, 132038, 132058, 132085, 132107, 132114, 132119 and 132120.

FJ-2 IMPRESSIONS
By — Lt. Col. Hondo Frain, USMC, ret.

I entered flight school in July 1952, and received my wings in Dec. 1953. From there, I entered jets, flying F9F-2s at NAS Kingsville. After finishing training in Texas, I was transferred to MCAS El Toro, where I entered a squadron staffed with ninety pilots and zero planes. Another squadron on base, VMF-235, had the new North American FJ-2 Fury. Apparently, when the squadron first received the FJ-2 Fury, some first tour pilots were attached. Well, someone in his infinite wisdom decided we couldn't have these new pilots flying our hottest airplane and transferred them out. So what you had were veteran combat pilots, Captains, Majors, Lt. Cols. and Cols. flying the dash 2. Soon after I arrived in Calif., this decision was rescinded and 25 of the vets were transferred out to form the nucleus of other Fury squadrons. This left room for 25 of the happiest Lieutenants in the Marines.

I remember the FJ-2 as the most fun, best airplane I ever flew, because at the time it was the dream airplane and window to the future. I have to say I had a relatively uneventful tour in the dash 2.

Transition to the FJ-2 consisted of a one week ground school, to learn the aircraft's systems, then a blindfold cockpit check, and then start her up and take off. I entered the squadron in June 1954 and shipped out for Japan in December. I think the average flight time, when we left the states, was 20 to 25 hours. Proficient we were not.

However, we did get a chance to learn how to shoot with the FJ-2. The first few flights none of us could hit anything when attacking a banner, but the Col. could get 200 banner hits. We then started putting in gun camera film and found out that if you fired at 600 to 800 feet instead of our usual 1200 to 2000 feet you could hit something. It wasn't as accurate as a F-9, where a good pilot could hit about 60%, but with practice you could score 40%.

Mechanically we had two problems with the airplanes. These were flight control and engine problems. The FJ-2 was one of the first aircraft with an irreversable hydraulic system. One speck of dirt or water or any other contaminate and the ailerons would freeze. The engine problem resulted from the engine throwing turbine blades. This problem was finally corrected by redesigning the attachment points of the blades into a christmas tree affair. These problems would cause us or VMF-451 to lose one airplane a month. J.B. Hanes scratched two planes. The first crash occurred when he had experienced a radio failure. Hanes then stayed in the pattern, and proceeded to have an electrical failure, then a hydraulic failure and finally an engine failure which resulted in his aircraft running off the edge of the runway.

Drop tanks were a necessity on the dash 2, unlike the FJ-4 to come. Internally 27,000 lbs. of fuel was carried. This was enough to fly to 40,000 ft. turn around and come home. So most of the time we flew with drop tanks, but without them it was one fun airplane.

PHOTO BELOW — Four VMF-235 FJ-2's over Japan. Photo via Bob Kowalski

PHOTOS: ABOVE — Business end of a FJ-2. Note open access doors and folded wings. **BELOW** — A beautiful VMF-235 FJ-2 after just getting washed. Photos by Nemila via Clay Jannson, Oct. 1954.

PHOTOS AT RIGHT: TOP — FJ-2 and F9F-6 of VF-24, coming up on the #2 deck edge elevator on board the USS Hancock (CVA-19) during project steam flight operations off the coast of San Diego, Calif. on 14 July 1954. **MIDDLE** — Maj. F.C. Thomas launches in #22, from CVA-19 on 22 June 1954. **BOTTOM** — Major. Thomas recovering in 131979. Note fin tip is painted grey above the red stripe with white stars. National Archives photos.

PHOTOS: TOP — VMF-235 FJ-2 piloted by Capt. W.R. Quinn is launched from the starboard catapult of CVA-19 on 1 July 1954. National Archives photo. **BELOW LEFT** — 131990 is hoisted aboard the USS Corregidor for shipment to Japan. Note aircraft were given a preservation coating to prevent corrosion during the trip. **BELOW RIGHT** — Fantail of Corregidor with two VMF-235's FJ-2s and one VMF-451 FJ-2. Photos via Clay Jannson.

PHOTO ABOVE — Two VMF-235 FJ-2s flying top cover. 12/WU is 131987 and 6/WU is 131990. Copy photos via W.T. Larkins.

PHOTO BELOW — 131965 at the El Toro flightline in 1954. 2nd Lt. L.F. Sledge is written under canopy. Photo by Clay Jansson.

VMF-312

VMF-312 was commissioned on 1 June 1943 and flew the F4U-1 Corsair. The squadron went on to fly the F7F-3 Tigercat, F4U-4/4B Corsair, F9F-4 Panther, FJ-2 and FJ-3/3M Fury, F8-A/E Crusader and the F-4B/J Phantom.

In Nov. of 1954, while stationed at MCAS Cherry Point, the squadron deployed the FJ-2 Fury. The FJ-2 was replaced two years later by the FJ-3/3M Fury. While flying the dash twos, the Checkerboards deployed to Roosevelt Roads, Puerto Rico for two months of gunnery and tactics exercises, begining in Feb. of 1955.

FJ-2s assigned to VMF-312: 131936, 131943, 132046, 132050-132057, 132059, 132061, 132063, 132064, 132068, 132074, 132078, 132088, 132090, 132091, 132093, 132094, 132096, 132097, 132105, 132106 and 132108- 132110.

PHOTOS: ABOVE AND BELOW — Two views of FJ-2, 132110, in Jan. 1955. The checkerboard stripes are black and white, see front cover. Nose stripe is also black, although some VMF-312 FJ-2s have been seen with black on one side and white on the other. Photos by Balough via Menard.
AT LEFT AND AT RIGHT — Two views of 132093, one with fresh paint, one with faded. Photos by G.S. Williams via W.T. Larkins.

1. Right Wing Formation Light (Green)
2. Right Wing Position Light (Green)
3. Right Fuselage Formation Light (Amber)
4. Left Wing Position Light (Red)
5. Left Wing Formation Light (Red)
6. Landing Light (Clear)*

7. Approach Light (Red, Green, Amber)
8. Lower Fuselage Signal Light (Clear)
9. Upper Fuselage Signal Light (Lunar White)
10. Left Fuselage Formation Light (Amber)
11. Tail Position Light (White)

* AIRPLANES 132047 THROUGH 132126 AND AIRPLANES HAVING SERVICE CHANGE NO. 128 COMPLIED WITH

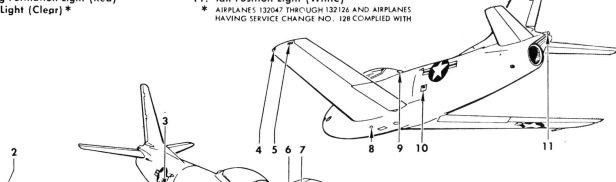

EXTERIOR LIGHTS

PHOTO BELOW — VMF-334 FJ-2 132055 in May 1955. Lightning bolt is red, stylized bird on fuselage and tail is black. Photo by Fahey via W.T. Larkins.

FJ-2s assigned to VMF-334: 132013, 132044, 132045, 132047, 132048, 132055, 132066, 132069-132072, 132075, 132079, 132082-132084, 132086, 132089, 132092, 132095, 132102, 132104-132106, 132111, 132116, 132117 and 132125.

VMF-334

38

VMF-451

The Warlords of VMF-451 were commissioned in 1944 and flew F4U-1 Corsairs from CV-17, USS Bunker Hill in 1945. The squadron then went on to fly F9F-2 Panthers and then FJ-2 Furys at MCAS El Toro in 1954. VMF-451 would later deploy its FJ-2s along with those of VMF-235 at NAS Atsugi, Japan. The Warlords then traded in their FJ-2 Furys for FJ-4 Furys, thus becoming the first Marine FJ-4 squadron. VMF-451 would go on to fly F-8 Crusaders and in the late 60's they would become known as VMFA-451, flying the F-4 Phantom.

FJ-2s assigned to VMF-451: 131941, 131950, 131962, 131964, 131973, 131974, 131978, 131982, 131983, 131993-131995, 131999, 132001, 132004- 132012, 132016, 132019, 132025, 132026, 132029, 132033, 132034, 132036, 132100, 132113, 132122 and 132126.

PHOTOS: ABOVE — VMF-451 flightline at MCAS El Toro on 15 Oct. 1954. Note that this is an early photo, as the aircraft have only a blue tail stripe. 131995 is in the foreground. **BELOW** — Two photos of VMF-451 FJ-2s being loaded aboard the USS Corregidor for shipment to Japan. Photos by Clay Jannson.

PHOTOS: ABOVE — Four VMF-451 FJ-2s in flight. Note that complete markings have been applied. Nose, fuselage and tail stripe are blue with white stars. USMC photo. **BELOW** — VMF-451 FJ-2s, side #s 1, 2, 3, 4, on taxi-way at MCAS El Toro in Sept. 1954. Photo via Clay Jannson.

The following FJ-2s were assigned to the indicated units. FAGU (fleet air gunery unit) 132015, 132018 and 132034. Hedron 17, 132015 and 132034. H&MS-32, 132042 and 132065. HU-2, 132029. **PHOTO BELOW** — H&MS-32 FJ-2 132065 in Sept. 1955. Fuselage and tail stripe is blue with black arrows. By D. Lucabaugh via Picciani Slides.

SUPPORT UNITS

Fuselage and tail stripe is blue with black arrows.

THE RESERVE FJ-2
As remembered by Captain Dudley Gillaspy

I entered reserve squadron VF-921, at NAS St. Louis Mo., in the spring of 1957. I was fresh out of the fleet with about 1500 hrs. of jet time, so I was really a "Welcome Soul". The squadron was just transitioning to the FJ-2, and the average pilot time was about 15 hrs. in type. I was given a start card and an emergency procedure card, and then one of the pilots stood on the wing and talked me through the start — from there on it was "catch me if you can." When I returned to base 1½ hours later — "I are a FJ pilot."

Unfortunately St. Louis was not the best base to operate out of. We were unable to get as much flight time as we would like, because the heavy traffic caused us to sometimes burn as much as 25% of our fuel before we got airborne. NAS St. Louis shared the runways with heavy civilian, commercial and military traffic from McDonnell. Because of this congestion we also flew with drop tanks of the 120 gal. variety. Even with the drop tanks our birds had short "legs", about 700 to 800 NM cross country was our maximum range.

I remember the FJ-2 as having a tendency to do what we called the "JC" maneuver or nose pitching up and down from overcontrol. Especially if you had been used to flying with a neutral hands off and then attempted minor attitude changes. We found the best remedy to be to trim just a flick nose down from neutral and let the stick have just a small bit of forward pressure. This was especially good in formation flying.

The only chronic mechanical problem we had was transferring the fuel from the drop tanks to the midcell. You really couldn't tell whether you had all the fuel from the external tanks transferred when the indicator light went out. Several times an aircraft landed with one tank dry and one full, in which case landing stability could be a real Bitch. We even had a plane drag a wing-tip and tank on landing due to a full drop tank on only one side. Therefore good fuel management became a trademark of the squadron.

My experience flying the FJ-2 was relatively short. I had accumulated about 75 hours in type when OPNAV shut down St. Louis in late 1957.

ST. LOUIS

ST. LOUIS FJ-2s were painted three different ways. **TOP** — 131942 in grey and white scheme with orange reserve band, black anti-glare panel and red intake warning. 132040 in orange and white with ST. LOUIS under NAVY and red intake warning. **AT LEFT** — 132010 in natural metal with orange fuselage stripe. **BOTTOM** — 132086 and 131954 in orange and white. Note white intake warning and that wing tanks are half black on the inside side. Natural metal leading edges. 1957 photos by Balough via Menard.

The following FJ-2s were operated at ST. LOUIS — 131932, 131935, 131937, 131942, 131945, 131949, 131951, 131953, 131954, 131957, 131960, 131961, 131962, 131969, 131976, 131990, 131995, 132007, 132010, 132019, 132040, 132045, 132048, 132053, 132066, 132070, 132083, 132086, 132092, 132101 and 132102.

COLUMBUS

PHOTOS: TOP — 131954 in orange and white scheme with natural metal leading edges, black anti-glare panel and white intake warning. Photo by Gelbubous via W.T. Larkins. **MIDDLE** — 131986 natural metal with orange reserve strip, black anti-glare panel and red intake warning. Photo by McLean via W.T. Larkins. **BOTTOM** — 131976 on 3-21-60 at NAF Litchfield Park. Note blue drop tanks. Menard photo.

Bogus F-86, a FJ-2 Fury painted as a memorial for Lt. Hard of the 44 FBS, Sabre City Trailer Park, No. Highlands, Calif. via Menard.

THE FJ-2 IN PLASTIC

Since the third XFJ-2 prototype was just a F-86E with four 20mm guns and other minor modifications, the Monogram F-86 in 1/48 scale and the Heller F-86 in 1/72 scale make perfect choices for this aircraft. Modifications needed on the Monogram kit to make #756 are the removal of the wing fences and scoop on the right side of the fuselage under the speed brake. Also the six guns ports have to be filled in and new gun-ports made for the cannon.

Note that guns were mounted lower on the XFJ-2B than on the production FJ-2s. Also the gun access doors will have to be filled and then recut; in addition the XFJ-2B used a different nose wheel than the F-86. The Heller kit needs the new wheel and the same gun port and gun access door surgery. For this book the Monogram kit was used for the XFJ-2B and the Heller kit was built up stock with kit decals to depict the Mig Mad Marine on Air Force exchange duty.

Lindberg has also produced a FJ-2 model in 1/48 scale dating back to the early 1950s. It is currently available in bogus markings of VF-51. The kit is crude by today's standards as it has no wheel wells, no cockpit detail save a crude pilot and is a motorized model, which means many holes in the lower fuselage which need to be filled. Except for an incorrect intake and forward canopy shape, the outline is acceptable for a kit made 30 years ago. Our kit was built as the second prototype, XFJ-2 133755, using decals printed by IPMS. The holes in the bottom fuselage and wings were filled and the kit was built in the flight mode with cockpit detail, an acceptable pilot figure, and wing-tip probes.

Note that the three XFJ-2s all had horizontal tail surfaces with dyhedral, like the F-86s.

ESCI/SCALECRAFT have produced a 1/48 scale FJ-2/FJ-3 kit. The kit comes with decals for a FJ-2 of VMF-451 and a FJ-3 of VF-154. Parts for the FJ-3 which are not used on the dash two are wing fences and dorsal fuselage cooling scoops. We built up one kit stock from the box with the kit decals. The kit has some major short comings, mainly centered around the nose section. The canopy shape and nose intake area aren't even close, and if you look at the photos of the models you will see it takes on a comic book appearance. Another problem area is the rear exhaust. Also missing from the kit are the fuselage cooling holes located where the scoops would be attached on the FJ-3.

In order to build a proper FJ-2, we took the Monogram F-86 fuselage and modified it to the FJ-2 configuration. This was done by cutting the cooling holes, adding vertical stabilizer fairings from the ESCI kit, using ESCI horizontal stabilizers, using ESCI tail bumper, making arresting hook, reshaping intake to FJ-2 configuration, filling F-86 gunports and cutting FJ-2 gun-ports, modifying forward windscreen area to accept cut down ESCI windscreen and finally adding complete wing and landing gear from ESCI kit. Model was then completed using markings from Microscale sheet #48-129, which provides decals for a VMF-235 and a VMF-312 airplane. VMF-235 was chosen.

PHOTO BELOW — Although not a FJ-2, the NAVY currently uses QF-86Fs and QF-86Hs. This photo depicts QF-86F 555017 as made from the crude Matchbox F-86A kit.

THE QF-86

QF-86F, Pt. MUGU Calif., silver paint with blue tail stripe and blue and gold PMTC emblem. Circa 1980.

QF-86F, 555087, Pt. MUGU, markings same as above plus red tail flash and outer wings. Circa 1981.

QF-86F, 53849, silver paint, turbine blade stripe is red. Circa 1982.

QF-86F, 562814, ex Blue Impulse aircraft in distinct blue and white markings. Circa 1982.

QF-86H, 522090, SEA camouflage with new metal fin, red and white fuselage and wing tip stripes and nose. 1977.

QF-86H, 531409, silver with black fin tip, red fin stripe, red and white fuselage and wing tip stripes, nose bottom red with top white. 1977.